T0131366

SUCCESSIONS

SUCCESSIONS

MICHAELA DI CESARE

PLAYWRIGHTS CANADA PRESS
TORONTO

For professional or amateur production rights, please contact:
Ian Arnold at Catalyst TCM
15 Old Primrose Lane, Toronto, ON M5A 4T1
416-568-8673 | ian@catalysttcm.com

LIBRARY AND ARCHIVES CANADA CATALOGUING IN PUBLICATION
Title: Successions / by Michaela Di Cesare.
Names: Di Cesare, Michaela, author.
Description: A play.
Identifiers: Canadiana (print) 20210393424 | Canadiana (ebook) 20210393440
  | ISBN 9780369103444 (softcover) | ISBN 9780369103451 (PDF)
  | ISBN 9780369103468 (HTML)
Classification: LCC PS8607.I2125 S83 2022 | DDC C812/.6—dc23

Playwrights Canada Press operates on land which is the ancestral home of the Anishinaabe Nations (Ojibwe / Chippewa, Odawa, Potawatomi, Algonquin, Saulteaux, Nipissing, and Mississauga), the Wendat, and the members of the Haudenosaunee Confederacy (Mohawk, Oneida, Onondaga, Cayuga, Seneca, and Tuscarora), as well as Metis and Inuit peoples. It always was and always will be Indigenous land.

We acknowledge the financial support of the Canada Council for the Arts, the Ontario Arts Council (OAC), Ontario Creates, and the Government of Canada for our publishing activities.

Canada Council for the Arts · Conseil des arts du Canada

ONTARIO ARTS COUNCIL
CONSEIL DES ARTS DE L'ONTARIO
an Ontario government agency
un organisme du gouvernement de l'Ontario

Canadä

ONTARIO CREATES | ONTARIO CRÉATIF

For Gab, who hoisted me up on his shoulders so I could reach the best spots for my Montreal Fringe posters twelve years ago, and who continues to lift me up every day.

FOREWORD
BY TAMARA BROWN

A curious phenomenon exists in stories in that the more specific in detail and perspective they are, the more universal they feel; what we may believe to be our most singular and private experiences are often the very ones that unite and resonate within us all. To me there is nothing more universally human than a story—they reflect the other back to ourselves and can act as a conduit for learning and connection in the way they speak to who we are, where we've been, where we're going, and even to who we hope to become. A story can be the shortest distance between people; it's difficult to hate and fear the other once we recognize their story within ourselves. We may be singular, but we are not alone.

It's understood that a homogenous Canadian experience or identity doesn't exist, and yet it can be argued that most of what is considered Canadian cultural canon disseminated on our stages, screens, and in literature is often confined to a depiction of humanity that reinforces the image and primacy of the Canadian colonial identity. As a director, I am most attracted to stories that feature the complex humanity and diversity of the lived experiences of marginalized people or communities who do not typically see themselves represented beyond the tropes and stereotypes that are associated with them in society. There is a particular music that has emerged as a result of the lived experiences and culture specific to my neighbours from the Italian diaspora in Montreal. Its refrains are hauntingly familiar to any other community who has also come to participate in the Canadian colonial project, depending on their perceived proximity (or not) to whiteness and respectability politics.

The significance of Michaela Di Cesare's voice as a playwright is about so much more than being a trailblazer of representation for her community, it's also in the point of view she brings to her storytelling: an unabashed, feminist gaze that is as compassionate as it is unflinchingly honest and irreverent in its regard, tinged with a dark sense of humour that is an act of resistance, provocation, and release, but also one of hope.

Throughout the workshop and up until the time of production, my imagination was captured by the play's larger questions of cultural/societal and ancestral/familial legacies in all their forms: the ways in which they impact the events of our lives, the stories we tell about ourselves, and of the belief systems and behaviours we inherit occupying as much space in our lives as a house crammed full of physical possessions. Three years after its world premiere in Montreal, the simple, inevitable, and difficult truths about grieving found in *Successions* are particularly resonant during a global pandemic—the messiness of change that it provokes, the tug of war between hope and despair, the flashes of clarity or questioning that arise, and how the bonds that tether us to the world around us are either forged or broken as a result. I've certainly come to a far more intimate understanding of what it is to grieve the death of a parent and to sort through a lifetime of personal belongings far sooner than I ever expected or wanted. In the story of Anthony and Enzo Di Ciccio, Cristina Tommaso, and Nat Trimonti, I am struck anew how life continues inexorably alongside death without any pause or consideration of the space and time needed for grief to become manageable, of how little time and space the brothers have in which to unpack a lifetime and decide how to move forward from there, and all the ways that hope fuels the entire process.

Successions reminds us all that we too have the choice to either accept or to renounce the legacies that shape our lives and identities and to what extent— hopefully with our hearts and sense of humour still intact.

Tamara Brown is an award-winning multidisciplinary performing artist, creator, and poet based in Montreal who acts, sings, and directs for both stage and screen. An occasional educator and perpetual student with a love for storytelling, natural sciences and the environment, alchemy, geekery, harmony, and social justice, Tamara is one of the founding members of Metachroma Theatre, created to address the under-representation of IBPOC artists in Quebec and Canadian theatre since 2010. In 2019, Tamara wrote Blackout *for Tableau D'Hôte Theatre with Lydie Dubuisson and Kym Dominique-Ferguson. Her work as a director has been seen on stages in Montreal, Toronto, Sherbrooke, Winnipeg, New York, and Stratford.*

Successions was first produced by Centaur Theatre, Montreal, from April 10 to May 6, 2018, with the following cast and creative team:

Enzo: Davide Chiazzese
Anthony: Carlo Mestroni
Nat: Gita Miller
Cristina: Tara Nicodemo

Director: Tamara Brown
Dramaturg: Micheline Chevrier
Set and Costume Design: Diana Uribe
Lighting Design: Audrey-Anne Bouchard
Stage Management Team: Melanie St-Jacques, Samira Rose, and Merissa Tordjman
Apprentice Stage Manager: Brandon Hepworth

A NOTE ON THE DIALECT

An accent typical among East-End Montrealers (especially but not limited to those with an Italian background) is used by Nat and Enzo. Anthony slips into this accent in his most emotional or off-guard moments.

It's not an American, Jersey Shore, or Brooklyn accent. It is its own unique dialect, as much influenced by French as by English and Italian. Sometimes I've written the dialect into a word, but most of the time I have not. Here are some useful tips:

TH = D, or remove the H depending on the word (e.g.: mother = mudder, third = turd)
ST = SHT (e.g.: street = shtreet) generally consonants in words are over-articulated
Mii = expression used for emphasis, shortened from the swear word *minchia*
Bey = expression equivalent to the shrugging of one's shoulders

There is a musicality to the dialect, alternating between a slow and fast tempo. Sometimes words are stretched (or shtretched), and sometimes they are clipped or melded into the next word in a sentence.

CAST OF CHARACTERS

Anthony Di Ciccio: forty, a lawyer turned politican.
Vincenzo (Enzo) Di Ciccio: thirty-six, a plumber, Anthony's brother.
Cristina Tommaso: thirty-eight, an actor turned campaign manager,
Anthony's wife.
Nat Trimonti: twenty-two, a beautician, Enzo's girlfriend.

SCENE

A bungalow in St-Leonard, Montreal

TIME

September 2019

The exterior of a typical St-Leonard bungalow, south of the 40, that has seen better days—much better days. The entire house is overflowing with belongings. The yard has a non-functional fountain, patches of dirt with old sticks where a garden once grew, and various objects strewn about. A cluttered basement can be seen off the garage. It is where all the "overstock" of three generations of an Italian family has ended up. There are elements of the '70s to it. There is a makeshift bar area, with lots of old bottles.

Mason jars and wine jugs are stacked beside Catholic relics. There is a large canvas painting visible amid the clutter. It is a portrait of a seventy-year-old woman with short silver hair and desperate eyes. The blinds are shut, leaving the room in darkness but for a streak of light on the painting, cast from between a set of broken blinds on one of the windows.

ANTHONY, an attractive man of forty, enters the basement. He is wearing a tailored suit and looks flawless. He can only make out the painting in the dark.

ANTHONY: Mom?

ANTHONY puts down his briefcase and stumbles to a light switch. He flicks it on. Nothing happens. He turns on the flashlight app on his phone and scans the room. Upon seeing the condition of the house, ANTHONY freezes.

CRISTINA, ANTHONY's wife, enters. She is slightly younger than he is and wears her business chic clothes almost as though they were a costume. She fits the role very well. She gestures to ANTHONY to show that she is on the phone. During CRISTINA's call, ANTHONY starts to have some difficulty breathing.

CRISTINA: Oh and send a note to the TLN interviewer. Make sure she doesn't introduce us as Mr. and Mrs. Di Ciccio. Or god forbid: Mr. and Mrs. Anthony Di Ciccio ... No, Cecily. You do not give a reason ... I would hope we were past the point of having to explain such a request. I'm a human with a name. My husband, the candidate, is a human with his own name ... Yeah. I know what optics are. I'm the campaign manager here ... No, of course you didn't mean ... Okay. Just confirm that we will arrive at the studio at four p.m. Thank you. And, Cecily ... don't forget ... Yes, perfect ... Bye.

CRISTINA hangs up. She also tries the light switch. She begins the arduous journey of walking around the mess and raising the blinds on the windows. ANTHONY still has not moved.

The interview is confirmed for four p.m. That should give us plenty of time to get these papers signed, grab lunch, and go over the talking points. Anthony?

She goes over to him, puts her hands on his face.

Hey.

ANTHONY wheezes. A bit pathetic.

Oh, honey. I told you—

CRISTINA fishes an asthma puffer out of her purse.

ANTHONY: No. Stop. I'm not.

CRISTINA: Yeah, yeah. You don't have asthma anymore.

ANTHONY: I don't. It's just the dust.

CRISTINA: So I should put it away then?

ANTHONY takes the puffer from her. He takes a couple of hits with his back to her and puts it in his pant pocket.

CRISTINA notices the painting for the first time.

ANTHONY: I knew they'd find a way to throw me off my game during the campaign. A classic "my parents" move. But this . . . they outdid themselves . . .

CRISTINA is staring at the painting. Beat.

Who was that?

CRISTINA: Who?

ANTHONY: On the phone.

CRISTINA: Oh, Cecily. She thinks I should take your name. I know that my family name can be a liability—

ANTHONY: She's your *assistant*. You already said no. Case closed. You have this pathological need to be liked by everyone at all times. Just shut it down.

CRISTINA: I do shut it down. She's stubborn!

ANTHONY: That girl was probably spoiled as a child. She doesn't take no for an answer.

CRISTINA: Woman.

ANTHONY: What?

CRISTINA starts to scratch an itch absent-mindedly.

CRISTINA: You called her a girl. You are infantilizing a grown woman, which in turn plays into the fetishization of young female bodies, which is just a skip and a toss from pedophilia.

ANTHONY: When in this conversation did I turn into a pedophile?

CRISTINA: My mother does it all the time. "I met this nice girl at the hair salon today." Turns out she's talking about a forty-five-year-old woman.

ANTHONY: *(checking his watch)* Have you seen my brother?

CRISTINA consciously notices the itch.

CRISTINA: I think something bit me.

ANTHONY: It's hives. You get hives as soon as we go east of Frontenac.

CRISTINA: Look who's talking. You get cranky within a two kilometre radius of St-Leonard.

ANTHONY: You grew up north of the Met. You don't understand the struggles we faced down here.

CRISTINA: *Poverino.*

ANTHONY: You're not reacting.

CRISTINA: To the bite?

ANTHONY: To what this place looks like.

CRISTINA: It's . . . as I expected.

ANTHONY: It's much worse than the last time we were here.

Beat.

It's been four years since you dragged me here for Nonno's wake, and in four years they managed to—

ANTHONY kicks one of the piles in a sudden burst of violence. Beat.

(motioning toward the stairs) Did you knock on his bedroom door?

CRISTINA: It was open. He's not here.

ANTHONY: Of course. Why would anyone related to me be dependable?

CRISTINA: He's not that late.

ANTHONY: No, not by our parents' standards.

CRISTINA: Here we go.

ANTHONY: They were an hour late to my first communion—someone else's dad had to snap my photo when I took the host; an entire day late for Christmas once, probably because they had to track down the gifts they forgot to buy; thirty minutes late to my swearing-in ceremony, which my father proceeded to sleep through.

CRISTINA: We always thought they'd be late to their own funeral.

ANTHONY: They weren't. Thanks to me.

CRISTINA: Don't.

ANTHONY: It's the truth.

CRISTINA: Your parents didn't even plan for things they knew were going to happen, like their next meal. This was—

ANTHONY: Stupid.

ANTHONY approaches some of the clutter

The civil code says we can only take clothing, personal papers—

CRISTINA begins to help him sort things.

CRISTINA: Souvenirs, trophies, medals, and perishables. I know.

ANTHONY: We're in and out in an hour. We make sure nothing's alive down here, Enzo signs the papers, we leave.

CRISTINA: Maybe throw in a few pleasantries. Nice weather we're having. How are you holding up? How's work?

ANTHONY: Work? Which work would that be? DJ, T-shirt designer, filmmaker—

CRISTINA: You know very well he's completing his plumbing apprenticeship hours.

ANTHONY: Yeah. We'll see.

CRISTINA: It means a lot to him. Resurrecting the family business.

ANTHONY: There's a reason it failed. Louie was awful at managing money and Enzo's the exact same way.

A car is heard pulling into the driveway outside. It makes odd sounds and comes to a clunking stop.

ANTHONY and CRISTINA listen.

ENZO: *(off stage)* Babe. I keep telling you. You need to jiggle the handbrake.

NAT: *(off stage)* You're just jealous your car likes me better.

ENZO: *(off stage)* I don't know a stick that wouldn't like you, babe.

Kissing sounds.

NAT: *(off stage)* I have to piss like a cow. Going upstairs. Here, take the pastries. And my snacks.

ENZO: *(off stage)* No prob, babe. I'll take the sweets. And the sugar.

More kissing sounds. ENZO enters.

Wey, there he is! The guy whose face is all over town. Nice posters. Your face is all, "vote for me or else."

ENZO places the food on the bar top.

ANTHONY: The electricity is off. And you're late. How can you be late? You live here. And how can you live here if there's no power?

ENZO puts the pastries and NAT's snacks (some chips, candy, and pop) down on the bar. He navigates the space with more ease.

ENZO: Uh, yeah, I'm trying to find the hydro bill. Daddy hid it somewhere. You know how he is.

ANTHONY: Uh huh. You live like this?

ENZO: Been sleeping at Nat's. She has a sweet condo, those new ones on Jarry.

ANTHONY: That's good. That you have a place to live. Other than here.

CRISTINA nudges ANTHONY.

The weather is nice.

ENZO: Yeah, it's hot as balls.

ENZO goes over and kisses CRISTINA on both cheeks.

Crissy.

CRISTINA: I love you. Don't call me that.

ENZO addresses the painting.

ENZO: Hi, Mommy.

ANTHONY: So that is a painting of Rita!

ENZO looks at CRISTINA. She looks away.

ENZO: Beh, yeah. You didn't recognize her?

CRISTINA makes eye contact with ENZO.

How's, uh, TV life?

CRISTINA: I'm dead now. On the show.

ENZO: Rough.

CRISTINA: No. I asked them to do it. It was the perfect time to focus on Anthony's campaign. I'm his campaign manager.

ENZO: *(imitating an Anglo accent)* Anthony.

(to ANTHONY) Minchia, so no one calls you Antonio anymore? Not even your wife?

ANTHONY: Where are the boxes?

ENZO: The boxes.

ANTHONY: We said I would draft up the documents and you would get boxes so we could do the triage of all this junk.

ENZO: Yeah. Yeah. I remember.

ANTHONY: That was your only job. While I performed my duties as liquidator of the estate, creating an inventory of the debts and assets of the estate, you were simply to go to Canadian Tire or Walmart or wherever it is people go to buy boxes.

ENZO: Home Depot. People go to Home Depot.

ANTHONY: Do you have the boxes or not?

ENZO: No, bro, sorry. But it's okay, we don't have to do that right away.

ANTHONY: Yes we do. That's why I'm here.

ENZO: Listen, Ant. There's some stuff I need to say.

ANTHONY gets his briefcase and is about to pull out some documents.

ANTHONY: Me too. I completed the inventory—

ENZO: Yeah. You've done a lot, uh, in the last couple of weeks that I couldn't, you know . . .

ANTHONY: Yes.

ENZO: And I can pay you back for the funeral stuff.

ANTHONY: Forget that.

ENZO: No. No. Let me pay half. I have money, bro. I just got a thousand bucks back from Rick, you know, that he owed me. And I have some savings—

ANTHONY: The funeral, the caskets, the burial plots, and the flowers cost $30,000.

ENZO just stares at him. He sniffs a couple of times.

ENZO: What did you, like, get the luxury package?

ANTHONY: It was the cheapest option Cristina would let me get. I suggested pauper's graves and setting fire to this place, but—

CRISTINA: So, Nat! That's the girl we met—

ANTHONY shoots her a look.

The woman. The young lady we met when we picked you up at Rouge . . . what was it, a year ago?

ENZO: Shit, that was the night we met. I went up to her like, "I'm a plumber so I can lay pipe real good." We had a blast until she got sick. Still can't look at Jäger without gagging.

CRISTINA: I didn't realize you were still together. She didn't come to the funeral.

ENZO: She couldn't come. Too many germs at a funeral.

CRISTINA: She's . . . germophobic?

ENZO: No! Haha. The opposite. She's a condom-phobe.

CRISTINA: Excuse me?

ENZO: We're pregnant!

Beat.

CRISTINA: What.

ENZO: Nat and me are gonna have a baby.

ANTHONY: The girl—the young woman—whose puke we had to get professionally cleaned out of our brand-new leather seats is going to be a parent?

CRISTINA: How old is she? I mean . . . she's younger than you, right? Quite a bit. Younger. And you've only been together—

ANTHONY: You didn't tell me. Why wouldn't you tell me something like this?

ENZO: I don't know, fuck. Maybe I wanted to postpone this piss-warm congratulatory reaction.

CRISTINA: Oh, Enzo. Congratulations. I'm sorry. We didn't . . . it's . . . we're surprised, that's all.

CRISTINA stares at ANTHONY.

ANTHONY: I need a glass of water.

ANTHONY exits upstairs.

ENZO: Ant, come on.

CRISTINA: He's really stressed—

ENZO: Yeah, what else is new? Mommy waited for you, at your usual time, every first Friday of the month.

CRISTINA: I couldn't keep coming here. We started working on the campaign together, so it was harder to slip away.

ENZO: You couldn't call?

CRISTINA: Enzo. I'm sorry.

ENZO: What the hell is a campaign manager?

CRISTINA: It's a lot of problem solving. And problem prevention. Making sure Anthony's image stays squeaky clean.

ENZO: Why wouldn't it?

CRISTINA: Enzo, did you tell anyone about what Anthony did?

ENZO: All three of us swore we wouldn't talk about it.

CRISTINA: Yeah, I know. And I trust you. But now that you have . . . someone special . . .

NAT enters the room. She is about eight months pregnant.

NAT: Your brother is banging around in the kitchen.

CRISTINA overcompensates by rushing to hug her. It's awkward.

CRISTINA: Nat, *bella*, look at you! You're glowing. Congratulations. Enzo just told us the good news.

NAT: Aw. Thanks.

CRISTINA: Wow, you're pretty far along.

NAT: Like eight months.

CRISTINA: Wow.

ANTHONY comes down the stairs.

ANTHONY: What you can't find in the kitchen: clean glasses. What you can find: every issue of *Good Housekeeping* ever printed.

ANTHONY sees NAT.

Wow.

NAT: Hi. Good to see you. My condolences by the way.

CRISTINA gives ANTHONY a look.

ANTHONY: Congratulations.

Beat

Nice weather.

NAT: Oh, the pastries!

NAT goes to the bar and starts arranging the food.

ENZO: Nat had the idea to stop at a pastry shop. We thought we could have a bite together before—

ANTHONY: No. Stop.

CRISTINA: We, uh, don't eat gluten. Or refined sugar.

NAT: Oh. I should have got something healthy. Like bagels.

CRISTINA: We ate already.

ANTHONY: We have breakfast at six a.m. After our workout.

NAT: So, what, it's like lunchtime for you?

ENZO: I think there's still some prosciutto in the cantina.

ANTHONY: We don't eat cold cuts either.

CRISTINA: Nitrates.

NAT: There's probably cheese.

ANTHONY: No thank you. We should—

ENZO: Whattaya got against cheese?

CRISTINA: We're actually a non-dairy family.

ENZO: You're two people. That's not a family.

NAT: I can go get something else. Some salad or something.

ANTHONY: We didn't come here to eat!

CRISTINA: It's fine, really. You shouldn't be driving around needlessly.

NAT: Ha, yeah, okay. I've been doing all the driving.

ANTHONY: All the driving? Has my brother neglected to inform me he lost his licence again in much the same way he neglected to inform me he is going to be a father? You know what? I don't care. I'm going to organize the papers because that's why we're here.

ANTHONY goes over to an old desk and wipes it down with his pocket square. He starts laying down documents atop it.

ENZO: Relax, Sherlock. You're jumping to assumptions. This isn't fucking Arabia. Women can drive here, you know? Ask your wife, she's always posting that angry feminist shit on Facebook.

CRISTINA: I think it's a misconception that all feminists are angry.

NAT: I think feminism is stupid. I like doing girly stuff for Enzo. Like making sangwiches.

CRISTINA: That's not—

NAT: And women acting like they're superior to men—

CRISTINA: That's really not—

NAT: It's just plain offensive. What if my baby is a boy? Am I supposed to love him less?

CRISTINA: I'm sorry I offended you, Nat. Do you still work at a beauty counter?

NAT: Yeah. MAC in the Gals.

CRISTINA: Any new eye creams come in this week?

NAT: I don't know.

Pause.

I don't need eye cream.

ANTHONY: Let's split the tasks. Cristina, you round up photos. I'll search for personal papers—bills, tax returns, anything like that. Enzo, you handle trophies, medals, and awards.

ENZO: As if we have any of those.

ANTHONY: And, Nat, you can—

NAT: Oh my god. There's a massage chair!

ENZO: The Vibercize chair.

NAT settles in on the massage chair.

NAT: What's Vibercize?

ANTHONY: My parents ordered that off an infomercial. The chair vibrates all your fat off while you watch TV. No need to try to improve your life, just be lazy!

NAT gets her phone out.

NAT: This is going to be the best Boomerang selfie.

ENZO: That thing never worked. Daddy got so fat using it.

ANTHONY: Uh yes, because if something sounds too good to be true, it probably is. That's a lesson they never learned.

ENZO: It was worth a try.

ANTHONY: No. There's no shortcut to success. No easy button.

NAT: I'm trying to find the easy button on this chair.

CRISTINA: The power's cut, Nat. It won't work.

ANTHONY: This would be a lot easier if we actually had BOXES. What happened, Enzo, your credit card maxed out again?

ENZO: Jesus Christ. You're not even here ten minutes and you're lecturing already. You think I don't know anything. I can't do anything right.

CRISTINA: Of course we know you're capable of buying boxes, Enzo.

ENZO: Damn right I am.

ANTHONY: But you didn't buy the boxes.

NAT: It's because he changed his mind.

ENZO: I changed my mind.

ANTHONY: What do you mean changed your mind? From what to what?

ENZO: I just don't get why this is so rush rush! We could take more time going over the options.

ANTHONY: Do you know what "time" is, Enzo?

ENZO: Is this like a riddle?

ANTHONY: Time is the most precious commodity in the world. It is the great equalizer between the rich and the poor because everyone has a finite amount of time to spend. Lend someone money, you likely get it back, perhaps even with interest. Time, once given, you never get back. My time is my most valued possession and I don't easily forgive those who waste it.

ENZO: That whole speech took up a lot of "time."

ANTHONY: Cristina and I are doing an interview with TLN this afternoon.

ENZO: *Mii* Telelatino. Just cancel.

ANTHONY takes out his phone.

CRISTINA: You can't cancel! That's my job. And we are not cancelling.

ANTHONY is dialling furiously.

ANTHONY: I'm calling 1-800-Got-Junk.

CRISTINA: That's not an option and you know it.

ANTHONY: Hello? I've got junk. How soon can you schedule a pickup?

ENZO snatches the phone.

ENZO: Ant, just wait a second. I want to do this together.

ANTHONY: Give me my phone.

ENZO throws the phone into the junk. ANTHONY takes off his suit jacket, hands it to CRISTINA, and starts searching. NAT looks up from her phone.

ENZO: You are my brother, and we are going to go through this shit and reminisce and shit, okay?

ANTHONY: Why are you torturing me?

ENZO: Because I love you.

ANTHONY: This house literally swallowed my phone. Someone, call me!

CRISTINA: Nat, can you dial—

NAT: I don't have a line. Only data.

ANTHONY: Cristina, go use the phone in the kitchen.

ENZO: Phone line's cut, just like the power.

ANTHONY: Of course.

CRISTINA: It's okay, there's my phone . . . somewhere.

CRISTINA *makes her way to where she left her purse.*

NAT: Enzo, I bet you there's stuff here you never even knew you owned. It's like a jackpot!

CRISTINA *is derailed.*

CRISTINA: I don't know. They say if something hasn't been used in six months that's a good indication it should be thrown out.

NAT: That's stupid. The question should be, "Will I use this massage chair every day for the rest of my life?" Yes.

CRISTINA: Well, the thing with hoarding is you always think you're going to need the thing one day, in some kind of emergency.

ENZO: *Mii.* Hoarding. That's those people on TLC who keep their toenail clippings and shit—literal shit—in Ziploc bags. That's not us.

CRISTINA: Hoarding is a mental illness that disproportionately affects immigrant populations. A need to accumulate possessions to avoid feeling uprooted, to be prepared for the unexpected, and to have tangible goods as an indication of success . . . I researched for a character once.

ENZO: This one guy they showed on TLC was trapped for seven years. Trapped in his own junk, can you imagine? He was having a heart attack and the ambulance guys couldn't get him out!

NAT: Did he die?

ENZO: I don't know. I changed the channel.

ANTHONY: WE AGREED WE WERE MEETING TODAY TO DO TWO THINGS: SORT THE POSSESSIONS AND SIGN THE PAPERWORK. DO YOU REMEMBER? WE WENT OVER IT IN THE STUPID RECEPTION ROOM IN THE BASEMENT OF LORETO.

ENZO: Okay, a bit, yeah. But like with the signing, you said we would probably have to reject—

ANTHONY: Renounce.

ENZO: I signed something at the funeral already. Was that the reject papers?

ANTHONY: That was your permission to make me liquidator of the estate. I explained all this.

ENZO: Sorry. I didn't understand everything you said. It was an emotional time.

ANTHONY: I don't have time for emotion.

ENZO: Bro, I hope you're joking.

ANTHONY: Cristina, did you call my phone yet?

CRISTINA: Sorry, I—

ANTHONY: I need you to anticipate my needs.

    CRISTINA dials.

    ANTHONY's phone starts ringing (a normal ringtone) and he resumes his search.

ENZO: Look at me and have a conversation with me, Ant! Forget your phone for two seconds.

ANTHONY: In my line of work I need to be reachable at all times.

ENZO: What about when your family tries to reach you?

ANTHONY: Excuse me? Who is it that takes your calls in the middle of the night?

In searching for his phone, ANTHONY has unearthed a statue of Lady Justice. He is on his knees, holding it up and staring at it.

NAT: That's like a trophy . . . that was on the list, right?

CRISTINA: Anthony?

ANTHONY doesn't move.

ENZO: Do you want time alone with the lady statue, Ant?

ANTHONY gets up and slams the statue down on the desk.

ANTHONY: I'm leaving. Sign the papers on the desk. Mail them to me. See if you can do anything without me holding your hand for once. Get boxes. Put aside perishables, photos, personal papers, and clothing. Find yourself a suitable place to live—

ENZO picks up a lead pipe. He handles it like a lightsaber, complete with Star Wars *sound effects. He tosses another pipe at ANTHONY.*

They've done this before.

No.

ANTHONY drops the pipe.

ENZO: *(while swinging at ANTHONY)* Why'd you come in here acting like such a little bitch?

ANTHONY picks up the pipe and joins in. The brothers spar over the next few speeches. Slashes indicate a hit.

ANTHONY: As a "LITTLE BITCH," / it's my responsibility to remind you that your next court date is on February 19th. As a LITTLE BITCH, / it's also my perception that the ONLY / reason / you ever contact me is to have me solve your legal problems—

ENZO: Fuck / you and your lawyer shit. As if you contact me / for anything besides needing an errand boy, as if you want me to contact you more often. /

CRISTINA: Guys, someone's going to get hurt.

ANTHONY: My LAWYER SHIT / has kept you out of jail! Do you have any idea / where you'd be right now if it wasn't for me?

ENZO: Shut up. /

ANTHONY: Any more infractions / to add to the list?

ENZO ramps up the last few hits. He ends standing over ANTHONY.

ENZO: No one / forced / you / to help me.

ANTHONY lets go of his pipe, defeated.

ANTHONY: That's all it ever was with you people. Help. Help. Help. The tickets, the taxes, the bills, the creditors, the lawsuits, the feuds, the drama, your general existence on this planet. Help.

ENZO: That's what families do.

ENZO drops his pipe. ANTHONY gets up.

ANTHONY: Well, I'm done. I want to take all the energy I've poured into this place and use it to do good for people who'll appreciate me.

ANTHONY takes a hit from his asthma puffer.

ENZO: You think I don't appreciate you?

ANTHONY: None of you ever put any value on my intellectual labour.

ENZO: What about me taking care of Nonno after you took off? That's uh—

CRISTINA: Emotional labour.

ANTHONY: Emotional— Who was paying Nonno's CLSC bills?

ENZO: That's not the same as being here. I couldn't go to school or take a full-time job until Nonno died.

ANTHONY: Ah fuck, my shirt is torn. You always make me do such stupid things. This shirt cost more than your car.

CRISTINA: It's just a shirt.

ANTHONY: Some of us couldn't just ask Daddy for a new shirt because the old one was "so last week."

CRISTINA: Okay. I see we've moved on to being hard on me now.

ENZO: You can't shit on Cristina for coming from a good family when we all know that's the thing you liked best about her.

CRISTINA: Hey!

ENZO: Whatever "good family" means, because last I checked our parents never screwed anyone over in business to get rich.

CRISTINA: Where'd you hear that?

ENZO: Crissy, please. Half of Montreal knows.

NAT: Babe! Gummies.

ENZO goes to get some candy for NAT and brings them to her.

Don't lose focus, babe. You had something to say to your brother.

ENZO: I fuckin' love you.

ENZO kisses NAT passionately.

I'm not who you think I am, Ant. I saved some money. I have a career now. I was thinking I could make you an offer on this place.

ANTHONY: You can't.

ENZO: I'm telling you I can! Plumbers make so much money because everybody went to university and now nobody knows how to do shit.

ANTHONY: Just take a look at the documents. You'll see why you can't make an offer—any offer—on this place.

ANTHONY motions to the desk.

ENZO: Am I about to be lawyered? Should I call Saul? Eh, you get it? *Breaking Bad, Better Call Saul,* you know?

NAT laughs and gives him a high-five.

ANTHONY: Can you pay attention for five minutes?

ENZO approaches the desk and leans over the documents.

ENZO: What am I looking at?

ANTHONY: The inventory of the succession. It includes reports from the land registry, the bank, and Equifax—

ENZO: Uh huh.

ANTHONY: And the municipal eval for reference.

ENZO: For what?

ANTHONY: This house.

ENZO: All these numbers, that's, like, how much it's worth?

ANTHONY: That's one of the mortgages.

ENZO: One of...

ANTHONY: One of three.

ENZO: That's not possible. Who gave them all these mortgages? What's this ... the five-hundred grand?

ANTHONY: It's the total debt on the estate.

NAT: No way.

ANTHONY: It's the mortgages plus personal debt. Like credit cards, for example. And taxes. See here, this statement from Revenu Québec? The first thing we'd be responsible for are these back taxes.

> *Beat.*

NAT: Babe?

ENZO: This is my desk.

ANTHONY: What?

ENZO: My homework desk.

ANTHONY: Did you hear anything I said?

ENZO: *(to NAT)* We had identical ones. My dad built them.

(to ANTHONY) I know it's mine because you smashed yours to pieces and left it on the curb the day you moved out.

ANTHONY: It's brand new. You obviously never did homework a day in your life.

ENZO: Yeah, but I used it to stash my weed. And I just got this feeling. Like a fifth sense. There's weed in here somewhere.

NAT: Woah.

ANTHONY: Enzo, please focus.

> *ENZO opens a drawer and pulls out a Larousse French dictionary. In the middle is a dime bag. He pulls it out.*

ENZO: In the dictionary, bro!

NAT: That's at least ten dollars' worth.

ANTHONY: Put that away. It's too dry to smoke.

ENZO: Wanna bet? I can rescue this. I just need some lemon juice and Scotch.

CRISTINA: Why?

ENZO: The lemon juice to lubricate the weed. The Scotch to lubricate us.

ANTHONY: You think we're all just going to get wasted?

ENZO: Not all of us. Nat's pregnant. Come on, bro. For old times' sake. Remember me and you on the roof of Santa Cabrini?

ANTHONY: This is really not the right time.

ENZO: Do you old farts ever loosen up anymore?

CRISTINA: We do! But it's more of a Friday night thing and less of a ten a.m. on a Tuesday thing.

NAT: Are you admitting you do it?

CRISTINA: What are you doing with your phone? Recording?

NAT: *Candy Crush.* You're paranoid as fuck.

CRISTINA: We vape. His lungs can't handle the smoke.

ENZO: *Mii.* You even get high like a pussy these days.

ANTHONY: Enzo. It's important that I get your undivided attention before I need to leave.

ENZO: Bro, you of all people know my attention span is at its peak when I'm lit.

ANTHONY: We have an interview scheduled in a couple of hours!

ENZO: Okay, okay. Listen. You have one drink and smoke one joint with me and I'll sign your papers. No questions.

ANTHONY: End of discussion? We renounce.

ENZO: Yeah. Whatever you think is best.

Beat.

ANTHONY: Okay. Light it.

CRISTINA: Anthony!

ANTHONY: You know I have a very high tolerance.

CRISTINA: Yes, I'm so proud. But we have—

ANTHONY: Just back off.

CRISTINA: *(to NAT)* No photos.

NAT: Yeah, cuz my @beautywithnat Instagram followers really want to see the two of you.

CRISTINA: We're quite popular, thank you very much. I'm even thinking of doing Christmas cards this year. Like the Trudeaus.

NAT: I can do your makeup.

> *Beat. CRISTINA looks at NAT.*

ENZO: Everyone to Nonno's bar!

CRISTINA: Nonno's bar. Is that what you call it?

ENZO: He was a drunk and proud of it.

> *ENZO gets rolling papers out and goes to work. ANTHONY starts to rummage behind the bar. CRISTINA and NAT stare at one another awkwardly while ENZO is concentrating on his joints.*

CRISTINA: So. Uh. Boy or girl?

NAT: Don't know for sure, but my nonna says girl because my pee smells like artichokes.

CRISTINA: Your nonna?

NAT: My mom's Italian.

CRISTINA: Of course, yeah. I didn't mean . . . And you're craving candy. Is that a sign of something?

NAT: Yeah. That I love candy.

CRISTINA: Anthony and I have been juicing lately.

ENZO: You mean taking 'roids?

CRISTINA: No. Vegetable juices. Beet and rutabaga. Kale. That kind of thing.

NAT: Gross.   ENZO: Disgusting.

CRISTINA: It might be good for the baby. You know, to cut back on the junk food.

NAT: People are always on pregnant women's asses about what we eat. No sushi, no soft cheese . . . what in the crap is that? Women have been birthing babies since, like, Jesus. I think we have it figured out. And don't even get me started on the pregnancy dieters. But maybe I don't care cuz I didn't get fat. I just got these amazing tits.

ENZO gives one of her breasts a squeeze.

ENZO: Honk!

ANTHONY has placed a bottle of Scotch, some glasses, and a bottle of lemon juice on the bar.

All right, now we just sprinkle this shit. And roll.

NAT: And roll.

CRISTINA: Nat, you don't smoke?

NAT: No! Not cigs. There's all sorts of chemicals in there. But weed's okay for pregnancy. It's natural.

CRISTINA: I'm not sure—

NAT: First you get all judgy about my gummies. Now you wanna get on my case about weed? What kind of a feminist are you? Don't I have a right to choose what's best for Nat Jr.?

CRISTINA: Nat Jr.?

NAT: Why not?

CRISTINA: Why not indeed.

ENZO starts waving the joint in the air.

ENZO: She's lit!

ENZO hands it to ANTHONY, who takes a puff.

CRISTINA: Not for me, thanks.

CRISTINA settles down on a big bag of sand.

NAT: You do you, Crissy.

CRISTINA: Don't call me that.

The joint and liquor start being passed around. NAT doesn't drink, but she does take a few puffs.

ENZO: To Mommy and Daddy.

CRISTINA: To Rita and Louie.

ENZO: They're probably up there having a drink with Nonno.

ANTHONY: And he's probably still complaining that the older son didn't get his name.

NAT: Yeah! How come you're not Enzo?

ANTHONY: I was born on St. Anthony's day. Rita thought that meant something.

CRISTINA: It does. He's the patron saint of lost things.

ENZO: You were spared the name. You were spared everything.

ANTHONY: The name suits you better. You act like an Enzo.

CRISTINA: And now we have Nat Jr. on the way.

ENZO looks at the women. Beat.

NAT: We haven't decided for sure.

ENZO: I'm gonna teach the little guy everything I know.

ANTHONY: That should take about an hour.

ENZO addresses NAT's stomach.

ENZO: Like when you go to the water slides, you with me, kiddo? You can get in for free whenever, just follow Daddy's simple rules. You show up in a bathing suit, carrying a towel. Before walking in, you dunk a bottle of water over your head so you're all wet, okay? Then you put the towel over your left wrist where the admission bracelet would go. Bam! That's it. You just walk past security. If and only if they talk to you, you say you had to take some medicine that was in your car. Medicine. Gets them every time.

ANTHONY: Why wouldn't you buy your child a ticket to the water park like a normal parent?

ENZO: Principles. You gotta teach your kid principles instead of spoiling him. Look at Cristina.

CRISTINA: I was not spoiled! And what's wrong with me?

ANTHONY: You lack basic survival skills. She can't camp. She can only glamp.

ENZO: Was that in—uh—where was the last trip you took? Some Asian place? I saw you right after you got back, I think.

ANTHONY: Dubai.   **CRISTINA:** Martinique.

ANTHONY: Oh, right. But Martinique was just a long weekend type thing. Not a big trip.

ENZO: *Minchia.* You've been everywhere but here.

Beat.

Mommy and Daddy hadn't taken a vacation in, like, twenty years.

ANTHONY: Yeah, twenty-one years ago this summer. That's when they took out mortgage number two to fly us all to Calabria and prove to estranged cousins that they were better off than them. Living the Canadian dream.

NAT: You talk funny.

ANTHONY: Me?

ENZO: Yeah, what's up with your accent?

ANTHONY: My accent?

ENZO: You didn't used to talk like that. All Anglo or some shit.

CRISTINA: I did that. Whipped the St-Leo right out of him.

NAT: Whipped. That's kind of kinky.

ENZO: Bro, you sound generic now.

CRISTINA: I think he sounds smart.

ENZO: You saying we sound stupid?

ANTHONY: She didn't say that. But your assertion is what lawyers would call a reasonable inference.

NAT: What kind of a lawyer are you, anyway?

ENZO: A smart one, apparently.

ANTHONY: Commercial litigation, with a specialty in real estate law.

ENZO: Fuck, really?

ANTHONY: It's okay. Louie never figured out what kind of a lawyer I was. Every time I saw him, he asked if I had visited any criminals in jail that day.

CRISTINA: Rita once asked if I was worried that the murderers Anthony put away would get out and try to kill us.

ENZO: Yeah, I'm pretty sure they thought you were like one of those *Law & Order* dudes.

CRISTINA starts shifting on the sandbag.

CRISTINA: What is this? Sand?

ANTHONY: That belongs to the City of Montreal. It's stolen property.

CRISTINA: Sand?

ENZO: Oh shit. Yeah. Nonno Vincenzo used to bring us to Parco Pirandello late at night to steal the sand!

CRISTINA: Why?

ENZO: Because he paid enough in taxes, that's why.

NAT: Babe. I didn't know you were a sand burglar. That's badass.

CRISTINA: This is crazy. You have publicly funded sand. Anthony, this is the kind of dirt they can dig up on you.

She cracks up.

Get it? Dirt.

CRISTINA is killing herself laughing.

I need to get up.

ENZO: She didn't even smoke.

NAT: Or drink.

ANTHONY: She does that. She cracks herself up.

CRISTINA is looking at the painting.

CRISTINA: I think it's sad that she wanted to paint but her parents told her it could never be a profession.

ANTHONY: They were right. They brought her over here on a boat just so she could have a job. I'm the first in the family to even go to university. Pursuing the fine arts is the ultimate sign of privilege and wealth. It must be nice not to care about making money.

CRISTINA remains very still.

I didn't mean you. Obviously. You did well with your useless degree.

CRISTINA: Give me the joint.

ANTHONY: Cristina, you're not like me.

CRISTINA: What I lack in practice, I make up for in enthusiasm. Gimme.

ENZO: That's my big sis.

ENZO brings CRISTINA the joint. She takes a few puffs.

Anyway, Mommy got to be a medical secretary at Cabrini. That's pretty good for an immigrant. She was happy at her job.

ANTHONY: That or she was miserable at home.

CRISTINA: I can't imagine not doing the thing I love in order to do something that someone else says is more worthwhile.

NAT: Isn't that what you're doing right now?

CRISTINA: No—is that what you think? I chose this. Anthony's a feminist too. He was the only lawyer in his firm to have a male secretary. That's progressive.

ENZO: It makes sense. The sand. You need to know how to screw the system if you want to survive. Like, did you know if you wanna mail somebody a letter you can put their actual address as the return address. You don't put a stamp. What does the post office do? RETURN TO SENDER. It's true. I made friends with a mailman in physio.

NAT: You're such a genius, babe.

ANTHONY: Physio? You're not on CNESST again, are you?

ENZO: No! I told you I'm serious about finishing my hours. One thousand three hundred and forty-two out of eight thousand done. I'm gonna be a master pipe mechanic by the time I'm forty.

NAT: It's part of his five-year plan. I made a vision board.

ENZO: Anyway, who needs CNESST when you can take pat leave?

ANTHONY: Won't that delay your plan?

ENZO: No way I'm missing out on pat leave! I'm gonna stay here at home, work on you, *giardino* . . .

ANTHONY: I don't know why you have to be such a wop sometimes.

ENZO: You know I don't like that word.

ANTHONY: Social services are not intended to truly help people. It's a system designed to imprison them.

ENZO: You mean, like, welfare?

ANTHONY: Welfare is about making sure certain people are poor enough that they can't afford to live in nice neighbourhoods and just satisfied enough so they won't slit your throat for a slice of pizza.

ENZO: Pizza. We should order pizza.

NAT: I have two-for-one on my Foodora.

ANTHONY: A) Gluten. B) I was talking.

ENZO: Okay, fuck. Continue your lecture.

ANTHONY: Quebec socialism is not about giving everyone a chance to be equally happy. It's about making everyone equally miserable—except for the very wealthy. There is no middle class. You're either the elite or you're not.

ENZO: So, who are you? The elite or the *pezzente*?

NAT: Who caaares? No one even looks at that stuff anymore. These days, everyone starts out equal—it's the law—and you make your own choices from there. Like, how I'm the number one makeup artist because I can do a custom cat eye with a three-shade contour. I have to turn clients away. Every. Day. None of that has to do with my mom leaving me with her parents when I was three or ANYTHING to do with the fact that my nonna gave me the down for a sweet-ass condo. My skills are what they are without counting fuckin' privilege points or whatever.

ANTHONY: What?

CRISTINA: I think she's arguing that we live in a post-gender, post-racial, post-materialist society.

NAT: I was just saying that we get to choose who we become.

Somewhere in the rubbish, ANTHONY's phone starts ringing. The ringtone is Rihanna's "Work," or a similar female anthem. He dives for it.

CRISTINA: You're going to break your head!

ANTHONY is searching with no luck.

ANTHONY: It's Cecily's ringtone. It could be urgent. Why isn't she calling you?

CRISTINA: You have a ringtone for Cecily? You don't have a ringtone for me.

NAT: Who is Cecily? She sounds like a badass.

ANTHONY: She programmed it on my phone. I don't know—

CRISTINA: That's interesting.

ENZO: Who's Cecily?

CRISTINA: A recent university graduate with a crush on my husband, apparently.

ENZO: What?

ANTHONY: Cecily is Cristina's assistant on the campaign.

NAT: Is she hot?

CRISTINA: She's an intelligent and accomplished young woman.

NAT: That's not what I asked.

CRISTINA: She's attractive, yes.

ANTHONY: She works for us.

ENZO: Oh yeah. Just work. You're just "working late" all the time.

CRISTINA: What?

NAT: He has this thing with cheating. It's why we can never have a threesome.

ENZO: Anthony. This is your wife. She is a beautiful woman. Sure, she's getting older—

CRISTINA: Excuse me?

ENZO: But women are like flowers.

NAT: What? Oh my god, flowers die like super fast.

ENZO: No, that's goldfish. Anyway, the fucking point is, how dare you, Ant? What is this shit? Some chick calling your phone when we're having family time?

ANTHONY: She's not "some chick"—

ENZO escalates in intensity.

ENZO: Are you fucking her?

CRISTINA: Enzo!

ENZO: You gonna ruin everything for some slut? Throw it all away over a dumb cunt?

ANTHONY: Stop talking to me like that. Don't you talk to me like I'm—

ENZO shoves ANTHONY.

NAT: Babe, you're freaking out a bit, that's all.

ANTHONY grabs onto ENZO's face.

ANTHONY: Hey. Look at me. Who am I?

ENZO: You're the man of the house.

ANTHONY: That's right. And what do I do?

ENZO: You take care of us.

ANTHONY: Yeah. That's who I am.

ENZO: Why is she calling you so much?

ANTHONY: She calls me to discuss the campaign.

NAT: Okay. I gotta ask. What's this campaign? Like, I keep seeing your enormous face on the way to Rouge—

CRISTINA: You're still clubbing?

ANTHONY: It's an election, Nat.

NAT: No shit it's an election. I meant what kind of election.

ANTHONY notices that ENZO is still upset. He's agitated and seems anxious.

ANTHONY: *(doing a Barney Gumble impression)* Oh no, an election! That's one of those deals where they close the bars, isn't it?

ENZO: *(doing a Mr. Burns impression)* Ironic, isn't it, Smithers? This anonymous clan of slack-jawed troglodytes has cost me the election, and yet if I were to have them killed, I would be the one to go to jail. That's democracy for you.

The brothers chuckle and high-five one another.

CRISTINA: Who are they now?

NAT: It's old-school *Simpsons*.

CRISTINA: Oh.

NAT: So, Ant is gonna be mayor? Like Mayor Quimby.

CRISTINA: It's not a mayoral election. It's a federal election. For a seat in Ottawa.

NAT: A seat. Okay. Mayor sounds better.

CRISTINA: *(to NAT)* Anthony pleaded a big case at the Supreme Court last year. And he won.

ENZO: Oh yeah. That was cool. All my friends were like, that's so cool.

CRISTINA: He overturned a Quebec Court of Appeal judgment that allowed smoking in multi-unit dwellings. When the judgment banning smoking was published, all three major parties were vying to have this star represent them.

NAT: Wow. Look how proud she is.

CRISTINA: I am. Look at him. Can you believe he just turned forty? He's my work of art. My Galatea. My Eliza Doolittle.

NAT: Huh? Your what?

ANTHONY: Cristina, I've told you before. This shtick is very embarrassing.

ENZO: Better she gets it out of her system now than in the interview.

CRISTINA: I got his cholesterol down from 7.2—7.2 can you believe it? It was through the roof when we met—I got it down to 2.85. That's the dairy-free, gluten-free diet we're on. Plus, the speech coaching, the fashion consulting—

ANTHONY: Okay, Cris.

NAT: Sounds like you did a lot for poor little Ant from the wrong side of the Met. It's too bad he totally threw your career under the bus.

CRISTINA: Many women put their careers on hold when they want to have children. Why is it any different if I take a year or two off to assist Anthony in this transition?

ANTHONY: Right, and I made sacrifices to help her when she was just starting out as an actress.

CRISTINA: What sacrifices?

ANTHONY: No, I just meant . . . going to theatre stuff, sitting on boards . . . being civil to a lot of horrible people.

ENZO: This guy went to see so many fucking plays. When they started dating, I was like, "Bro, I hope you're getting some or it's not even worth it." And he was like, "Bro, she's a virgin!"

CRISTINA: You told him that?

ANTHONY: I don't recall . . .

ENZO: *Bey* yeah, we were smoking on the roof—

ANTHONY: I. Don't. Recall.

ENZO: Oh, you don't, eh? You forget every conversation we ever had in here? Just wiped it all clean from your head? Wiped the whole place clean.

ANTHONY: You think I don't know when I walk into a courtroom that I carry this place on my back? Do you know how many racist colleagues made Mafia insinuations, to my face, in court, when I was just starting out?

NAT: Racism? Is he joking right now?

CRISTINA: You mean prejudiced colleagues, Ant, not racists.

ANTHONY: What I mean is I had none of the advantages of growing up crooked—no money, no influence, no connections—but I had all the disadvantages of my Italian roots.

You know how many times they made me spell my name for the stenographer? "Maitre D-d-duh si-si-sicky-o" and I'm repeating Di Ciccio over and over. Finally, I started walking right over to the stenographer and handing her a business card. It's an advantage right off the bat to have an easy to pronounce francophone name—like Trudeau. Not to mention the nepotistic advantage.

ENZO: Oh my god. Your disadvantages. I'm so sorry that your ethnic name and your tan face are such fuckin' inconvenient inheritances. It's not like you inherited a disability—

ANTHONY: A neurological condition.

ENZO: Yeah. It's no surprise the brother with ADHD couldn't become a lawyer. And meanwhile you, you fuckin' stole my Ritalin to help you study for exams.

ANTHONY: Oh please. I told you, you could have got into any program— even med school at McGill—by playing the disability card. You chose to play the victim instead. You chose to be stoned all the time.

NAT: He's better when he's stoned.

ENZO: It's okay, Nat. My brother just has a chip on his shoulder because he didn't get into McGill. He had to struggle and speak French over at Université de Montréal.

ANTHONY: I could have got into McGill. I made it to the interview round. My grades were solid. There I was, nineteen years old, coming out of CEGEP. The admissions officer recommended I do four years of an undergrad for "life experience" and then reapply.

ENZO: That's all it was? You just had to take some extra classes?

ANTHONY: A whole other degree, Enzo. That costs money. And I didn't qualify for financial aid or scholarships because Rita and Louie's taxes weren't up to date.

ENZO: Yeah, but that was your dream, McGill Law.

ANTHONY: My dream was getting out. I needed the shortest path to writing the bar and then work, money, safety, stability. No way I was going to wait eight years for that. Life experience! They thought I didn't have life experience . . . and what could I tell them? That I was already raising a family, raising my parents, cooking, cleaning, sewing, working odd jobs, studying—

ENZO: It's really easy for you to shit on our childhood and talk about carrying it on your back. Really? Where? I don't see it. You were able to throw on a suit and leave us all behind.

CRISTINA: Anthony has problems too.

ANTHONY: Cristina—

CRISTINA: No. I'm tired of them always acting like you won the lottery. I don't know everything that went down here, but Anthony clearly has some post-traumatic stress. He has nightmares and panic attacks.

ENZO: Aw, poor you, Ant. That must be tough. You have bad dreams and panic attacks like a pussy.

CRISTINA: I don't agree with trivializing panic attacks and using a pejorative word for the female anatomy to further stigmatize and gender mental illness—

ENZO: What the fuck is she even talking about? Jesus, Ant. You make your wife believe we're such dirt. Mommy and Daddy were not the worst parents in the world. They didn't gamble away our house or get divorced.

ANTHONY: Look around you! This was their addiction. And they should have divorced. That's what I wanted.

CRISTINA: It wasn't your decision to make.

ENZO: Step-parents suck, Ant. We would have been molested. Locked in closets and shit.

ANTHONY: Or maybe we'd still have all the money Dad spent as penance for his sins.

ENZO: We were poor. You don't get to be angry just because we were poor.

ANTHONY: We shouldn't have been. That's the point!

ENZO: Nonno got sick. Daddy had to close the business and start working for other companies. They had bad luck.

ANTHONY: There is no such thing as bad luck! Not here. Not in Canada. You make your own luck.

NAT: Yup. Hashtag self-made.

ANTHONY: In any other country they would have starved to death a long time ago.

ENZO: But what's the big fuckin' deal? We had food. We had clothes. We had a roof. We were fine. You were the one, fuckin' eighteen years old, sitting on the floor of the closet crying because you couldn't handle . . . what? I don't even know . . . being good at everything?

ANTHONY: You don't know. You were always protected from everything because you had a "learning disability." You know, getting stoned and never studying.

ENZO: Ah shut up, you were so jealous of me you went and invented your own "disability." You couldn't even let me have that.

ANTHONY: What?

ENZO: You fuckin' started pretending you couldn't see people.

ANTHONY: I didn't make that up.

ENZO: You gave it some bullshit name. Prissy piss whatever.

CRISTINA: Prosopagnosia.

ANTHONY: Cristina.

NAT: Pro-so-what?

CRISTINA: Face blindness.

NAT: You can't see my face?

    Beat. ANTHONY doesn't reply.

YOU CAN'T SEE MY FACE?

ANTHONY: I have a mild form of the neurological condition. I can learn faces I see often, but it's difficult. If I don't see someone for a while, I forget. Today, the only face I know by heart is the one I wake up next to every day—

    ANTHONY is being sentimental. CRISTINA cracks up.

CRISTINA: It's why he needs me at networking events! I'm such a cliché political wife, I need to whisper in his ear, "This is Maitre so-and-so."

ENZO: He was always calling my friend Tim, Sam and Sam, Tim.

ANTHONY: Tim and Sam went through a long phase of getting the same haircut and wearing the same clothes. Assholes.

NAT: Wait. Wait. What if you run into people, like on the street?

ANTHONY: It can get awkward, but there are other clues I can piece together: body size, gait, tone of voice, clothing.

CRISTINA: It's why he never noticed all his exes were ugly. Those girls benefited from his impairment.

NAT: *Mii.* And here she was a minute ago being all, "Blah, blah, female pussy power, blah, blah."

ENZO: Wait a minute . . . they were ugly . . . so this thing is real?

ANTHONY: Why would I make up such a stupid weakness?

ENZO: I thought you wanted to be more like me. For a change.

NAT: But, like, what do you see instead of a face?

ENZO: Babe, there's no instead of, there's just no face. Right?

ANTHONY: Not exactly.

ENZO: Like the Invisible Man. You just see hairstyles floating on top of clothes.

ANTHONY: No.

CRISTINA: There's a famous case of prosopagnosia where the man's brain replaced all faces with other objects.

NAT: Aha! So you do replace the face.

ANTHONY: In some cases.

CRISTINA: This man thought his wife was a hat.

ENZO: Do you think your wife is a hat, Ant?

NAT: More importantly, what kind of hat? I'd go with beanie.

ANTHONY: All cases of prosopagnosia are different! I do not see hat-people.

NAT: Then what do you see?

ANTHONY: It's sort of like . . .

CRISTINA: Lego people.

ENZO: What?

ANTHONY: The features are broad, cartoonish, kind of two-dimensional.

ENZO: Oh man! It's like you're living in Legoland. That's so cool.

ANTHONY: It's hard, Enzo. I always worry I'm going to ignore the wrong person. And I suck at non-verbal—what's the thing you always tell me, Cristina?

CRISTINA: Non-verbal cues. Subtle facial expressions are totally lost on him.

ANTHONY: Yeah.

CRISTINA: But I help. Those are kind of my specialty.

ANTHONY: Yet another thing for which I am indebted to you, right?

CRISTINA: I wasn't saying it like that.

ENZO: So, we're both kind of messed up, eh?

ANTHONY: It's all genetic.

CRISTINA: It's one of the many reasons we chose not to have children.

NAT: If one parent has ADHD, the kid has more than a fifty percent chance of having it too. So what? It's not like my kid will be retarded. We did those tests.

CRISTINA: I didn't say retarded. I wouldn't say retarded.

NAT: I'm sorry, but all you PC people. You hashtag-body-shaming people. You bully bulliers. You're really starting to get on my nerves. Being PC is just not saying true shit. I prefer to be honest.

ANTHONY: It's like how Rita got depressed all the time. It's something with the way the nerves work in our brains.

ENZO: No way. Depressed. What are you saying? She was just overwhelmed. She was working all day at the hospital, raising us, and taking care of Nonno. And he wasn't easy. The scratching, the yelling—he'd bite her sometimes.

CRISTINA: I saw him pinch her butt once.

ANTHONY: I begged her to get help. I guess in her own way, she finally did.

CRISTINA: What are you saying?

ANTHONY: Come on—the accident. Am I the only one who sees it?

ENZO: Dad fell asleep. He's been falling asleep at the wheel for as long as I can remember.

NAT: That's not a normal thing.

ENZO: He was always exhausted. He worked double shifts every day.

ANTHONY: . . .

ENZO: The point is he was a disaster on the road. The number of times he totalled the car by driving off the shoulder . . . it was kind of his thing.

NAT: He should have lost his licence!

ENZO: Nah, driving with him was always a blast! You'd just have Mom yelling at him to keep him awake, "Louie, ARE YOU ASLEEP?" And then he'd yell back, "WOMAN, YOU SCARED ME! YOU WANT ME TO DRIVE RIGHT OFF THE HIGHWAY?"

ANTHONY: I know he fell asleep. I'm not arguing that. I just think this time she let him. She thought up the perfect punishment for a horrible son like me.

CRISTINA: No.   **NAT:** She wouldn't have done that.

> *Beat.* CRISTINA *and* NAT *exchange a look.*

ENZO: Shit. Shit. That's fucked up. You're saying she just let him drive off the road? Jesus, fuck.

> ENZO *circles the room as though to clear the air and addresses the painting.*

Did you do that, Mommy? Did you let him? You let him?

NAT: You're upsetting my bae and my baby!

ANTHONY: It was just a theory. I—

ENZO: Why would you say something like that?

ANTHONY: Look, forget it. I'm buzzed, that's all. And I'm buzzed because I did what you wanted. We smoked, we drank, now please come take a look at the documents.

ENZO: Yeah. Okay. Whatever.

ENZO joins ANTHONY at the desk where the papers are.

ANTHONY: There is a grace period in which successors can renounce. Currently, we are in a holding period during which the succession is frozen.

ENZO: Oh. My. God. Remember Dash?

ANTHONY: Dash?

ENZO: Dash, the frozen cat.

ANTHONY: Oh, yeah.

NAT: You guys had a cat?

ENZO: Yeah, Dash—

ANTHONY: We had cats. Plural. My mother, despite her son's asthma, chronic bronchitis, and CAT ALLERGY took in every stray that turned up.

ENZO: You're telling it wrong. Fuck. Too many cry-me-a-river moments. So Dash, the cat, died in our house. It was winter so Daddy says he's going to go outside and bury him in the snow.

NAT: No.

ENZO: Yeah, and he even added a couple of shovelfuls of snow on top every day as the weather got warmer. So the cat's buried. Whatever.

ANTHONY: Yeah, whatever, we have six others at home.

ENZO: No. We had like two. Three max.

ANTHONY: Tell that to my collapsed lung, senior year.

ENZO: Oh shit, yeah, that was bad.

ANTHONY: One week in hospital.

ENZO: ANYWAY. Spring comes and the snow starts to melt. And you could start to see the stuff that was under there.

ANTHONY: Toilet seats, car engines, things Louie had long forgotten he even brought home.

ENZO: So we're coming home from school one day and we just see this thing sticking up out of the snow.

NAT: No!

ENZO: And we don't realize what it is yet.

ANTHONY: I did. You didn't.

ENZO: So I go pull on it and I pull up a fuckin' frozen cat. A whole cat that's still kind of in this block of ice—like a Popsicle.

NAT: Ew! Then what?

ENZO: Dad said to leave him there till everything was melted—

ANTHONY: Like that was his plan all along.

ENZO: And then he buried him in the actual ground.

ANTHONY: No. I did.

ENZO: You did not.

ANTHONY: Ask Lucy. She was watching from the window. As usual.

NAT: Lucy?

CRISTINA: Their neighbour.

ENZO: That stuck-up bitch always thought she was better than us. Always calling the cops on us.

ANTHONY: Does she still live next door?

ENZO: What do you think? As if that shut-in maniac would ever leave us in peace.

ANTHONY: She called the cops on our parents the night before my bar exam. Fucking sabotaged my studying.

ENZO: Do you have your campaign posters in your car?

ANTHONY: Uh . . . yeah.

ENZO: Let's put one on her lawn!

CRISTINA: NO! Bad idea.

ANTHONY: This is not even my riding.

ENZO: Come on. Let's show her who you've become.

ANTHONY: Enzo, it is illegal to put campaign posters up without consent.

ENZO: Okay. Okay. Not her front lawn. We can dump a bunch of them in her pool.

ANTHONY: Are you joking?

ENZO grabs the bottle of Scotch and ANTHONY's car keys off the bar and runs off stage.

ENZO: I have your keys!

CRISTINA: Oh no.

ANTHONY: Enzo! Stop!

ANTHONY runs after him.

CRISTINA: I should probably try to stop this.

She stares at NAT for a beat.

But I'm starving all of a sudden.

NAT: Good for you. Have some gluten.

CRISTINA picks up one of the pastries.

Ant said it was illegal to put the election signs up.

CRISTINA: Yeah ... technically.

NAT: Should I be worried?

CRISTINA: No. Anthony can talk his way out of anything. Or into anything for that matter.

NAT: Right. He bagged a virgin after all.

CRISTINA: What? Oh. Yeah. You know he . . . helped Enzo a few times. With the law.

NAT: Yup.

CRISTINA: Okay, you know . . .

NAT: About the big one, yeah.

CRISTINA: The big one?

NAT: I don't think it was that bad.

CRISTINA: You don't?

NAT: It's pretty funny actually. Humping a parked police car, pants down, yelling, "Fuck the police!"

CRISTINA: *(relieved)* Public sex with a police car. Yeah that, that's the big one.

NAT: Classic Enzo.

CRISTINA: Public indecency. Public intoxication. Threats against the police. You find that funny?

> *Beat.*

NAT: You don't like me.

CRISTINA: W-why would you say something like that?

NAT: Rita said you called me a drunk floozie. And yeah, okay, maybe I threw up in your car once, but you don't even know me.

CRISTINA: First of all, I may be older than you, but I'm not so old I would use the word floozie.

NAT shrugs.

You and Rita were talking?

NAT: Every day. She was excited about the baby. She gave me a scrapbook she made years ago to give to her first grandchild.

CRISTINA: She probably thought she'd be giving it to us. But, obviously, yeah. You're carrying the first. The only—unless you have others.

NAT: You can't?

CRISTINA: . . . I can.

NAT: It's okay if you can't.

CRISTINA: I can. I know I can.

Beat.

NAT: Oh. Sorry.

CRISTINA: No, don't be sorry. It's not a tragedy . . . we chose. I had just been cast on the TV show; it wasn't the right time. And we never wanted to be parents.

NAT: Anthony too?

CRISTINA: We're proud urbanite dinks.

NAT: Dinks sounds racist.

CRISTINA: It means double income no kids. It's in line with our politics.

NAT: Having or not having a baby is not a political statement.

CRISTINA: It should be. I'm going to say something extremist.

NAT: No judgment.

CRISTINA: Sometimes I want to start a feminist movement where women stop. Stop the baby-making. Go on a birthing strike. Because otherwise we can't have equality. The toll child-bearing takes on a woman's body and career—we haven't come close to evening out the playing field because at the end of the day the men will always be untouched, unchanged, unburdened. The stakes will never be as high for them. Putting aside everything else: ethics, overpopulation, pollution, global warming—motherhood is still the enslavement of women as incubators for the species.

NAT: Well, fuck.

CRISTINA: Sorry. I'm very high.

NAT: Rita also said you'd judge me about the baby.

CRISTINA: I would never judge a young woman faced with an unplanned pregnancy. And being pro-choice means I support—

NAT: This wasn't unplanned.

CRISTINA: You were trying to get pregnant?

NAT: See. You're judging.

CRISTINA: No.

   Beat

You're just so young.

NAT: Weren't you, like, a child bride?

CRISTINA: I was twenty-two.

NAT: I'm twenty-two!

CRISTINA: A baby is different. What about education, travel?

NAT: I'm not the one stepping aside for my husband's career.

CRISTINA: He deserves it! That man deserves to be someone's priority for once in his damn life.

NAT: Rita said she always put her sons first.

    CRISTINA laughs.

CRISTINA: And she was just misunderstood and if you knew the whole story you'd understand?

NAT: Yeah, that's what she said.

CRISTINA: When did the two of you get so close?

NAT: Over the last year. After you stopped visiting.

CRISTINA: Anthony doesn't know I was coming here.

NAT: No kidding. He's kind of a drama queen.

CRISTINA: You think?

NAT: What?

CRISTINA: That he's exaggerating about how bad things were?

NAT: How would I know? All I know is no matter what went down here, Rita stuck around. That sounds like a good mom to me.

CRISTINA: She stuck around... or she was stuck. Stuck here.

NAT: Deep.

CRISTINA stands in front of the painting.

CRISTINA: I wish there was a movie of his life that I could watch so I could see for myself... the truth of it. Rita would always say, "You can ask for the truth, but you'll never get it."

NAT: I see it now.

CRISTINA: What?

NAT: The tits, the waistline, the way your hips sort of slant—

CRISTINA: Excuse me?

NAT: The painting. Rita was always talking about how you sat for it ... perspective or something—

CRISTINA: Reference.

NAT: Yeah. I didn't understand what that meant until I saw you in front of it just now. It's your body.

CRISTINA: She always supported my art. She'd come to my plays and leave notes for me with one of the ushers. Sometimes there'd be a sketch of me in my costume with a quote. One of my lines. My parents don't even bother coming to see me anymore. So when Rita told me at Nonno's wake that she wanted to paint something and she needed my help, I couldn't say no. This is the last thing she ever painted. She called it "my truth for my sons."

NAT: What was she trying to tell them?

CRISTINA: That she felt outnumbered by men in this house. See how she's pulling down the collar of her dress to show a scar? When she was pregnant with Anthony, the doctors discovered something in her heart that needed to be operated on. In a way, he saved her life. But she'd say he became the person to cause her the most pain. That's what the scar represents.

NAT: But it's your chest.

CRISTINA: Technically. She thought we had similar bodies. Which, when you're married to a man who can't see faces . . .

NAT: Gross. Don't even finish that sentence.

CRISTINA: Your face is an important part of who you are.

NAT: Well, yeah.

CRISTINA: When we met it felt like love at first sight, except—

NAT: Except maybe he loved your brains and your personality. Fuckin' worst.

CRISTINA: Yeah. I mean, no. That's not what I meant.

Beat.

We eloped nine months after we met.

NAT: See, to me, that sounds like the crazier thing to do in nine months.

CRISTINA: I thought it was romantic. Anthony was very persuasive.

NAT: Were you really, like, an all-around virgin when you met Anthony?

CRISTINA: Before I met Anthony, I acted like my hymen was made of fucking Murano glass.

NAT: Enzo might be the last guy I screw.

CRISTINA: Is it really all that different with different people?

NAT: Oh, fuck yeah.

> *Beat.* CRISTINA *goes to the bar.*

CRISTINA: They took the Scotch away. Well, Nonno's vinegar wine will have to do.

> CRISTINA *drinks directly from the bottle.*

NAT: Do you ever see a hot guy and think you're missing out?

CRISTINA: No.

NAT: Never?

CRISTINA: Well. My spin instructor is very attractive. But I don't— You know, other than some invasive fantasies that I think are entirely due to the friction of the bicycle seat—

NAT: Oh my god. You are such a suburban stereotype.

CRISTINA: Take that back! We live in Outremont.

> CRISTINA *takes another swig from the bottle.*

NAT: Don't you have that interview real soon?

> *Beat.*

CRISTINA: She asked me if I thought a man who hated his mother could love any woman.

Beat.

I was sitting in the living room. In this tiny, claustrophobic space she had carved out by the window. Modelling. Not moving an inch. And she asked me that.

Beat. CRISTINA *drinks.*

It was the day Anthony and I decided to move ahead with the campaign. I promised to support him. I came here. I put on the dress. The painting was almost done. I told her I was going to leave the show. That Anthony was going to be running in the next election. And she didn't miss a beat from her paint strokes—she said, "Do you really think a man who hates his mother could truly love any woman? He makes you work to deserve his love, but it's never enough. Everything you do for him will be expected and everything he does for you will be a sacrifice."

Beat.

ANTHONY's *phone starts ringing.* Cecily's *ringtone.* CRISTINA *follows the sound to . . .* NAT's *massage chair.*

Why do you have Anthony's phone?

NAT: I can explain. They were making progress. If I was you, I'd be more worried that this bitch keeps calling your husband.

CRISTINA *gestures for the phone.* NAT *gives it to her.*

CRISTINA: What's your agenda here, Nat?

NAT: My agenda?

CRISTINA: You're being really pushy with Enzo. Putting all sorts of ideas into his head—

NAT: Me? More like your husband. Rita said Enzo always knows what he wants until he gets in a room with his brother and then he just gets bossed around.

CRISTINA: You have not been around long enough to say something like that. You have no clue. About anything.

NAT: I googled. Before when you were all arguing. I googled on the Quebec government website. The . . . successions page, that's what Anthony said, successions, and it says you always have a choice. It says:

NAT reads off her phone.

"The succession of a person opens by his death, at the place of his last domicile. A successor"—blah, blah—"is an heir from the opening of the succession, provided he accepts it. A person who renounces is deemed never to have been a successor."

A beat while she scrolls more.

AH, HERE, "Every successor has the right to accept or to renounce the succession."

So, why is the choice already made for Enzo?

CRISTINA: Anthony explains it all better, but—

NAT: Can Enzo keep the house or not?

CRISTINA: It's not the best course of action.

NAT: Why not? He wants it. And I want him to have what he wants. I want him to live here.

CRISTINA: Don't you want a fresh start for your baby?

NAT: I have my condo. I said I want Enzo to live here.

CRISTINA: Alone?

NAT: I love Enzo. But we only met last year, and I wanted a baby, not a husband. I need to go one step at a time. The first step is the baby. And, I don't know, I always thought we'd be married before we moved in together.

CRISTINA: You're a traditionalist. Sort of.

NAT: Tradition is good sometimes.

CRISTINA: The inheritance needs to be rejected because of the debt.

NAT: The five hundred grand.

CRISTINA: You really have been paying attention.

NAT: Enzo will figure it out. He's a hard worker. He'll work it off.

CRISTINA: Rita told me her entire salary from the hospital was going toward debt every month. How many custom contour eye things would you need to do to pay that off?

NAT: I'm not paying it. I just said—

CRISTINA: And then one day you realize all you're doing is paying into this bottomless pit of debt with everything that you have to give, and you can't even make a dent in it because you're paying for stuff you didn't even do— you're paying other people's debt, and there's *interest*. Don't forget about interest!

CRISTINA flails her arms and spills red wine on herself.

Ah shit. Ohhhh shit. Fuck. Fuck. Fuck.

CRISTINA runs up the stairs.

NAT: Where are you going? We were talking. And they say millennials are rude.

NAT follows her up the stairs, slowly. The stage is empty for a beat.

ENZO: *(off stage)* Screw you, Lucy! You're not better than us. You know who took a dump in your pool last summer? It was me!

ENZO and ANTHONY run back on stage, winded.

ANTHONY: Attention, womenfolk, we succeeded in confirming that Lucy still lives next door.

ENZO: I delivered a freestyle rap at her open window:

Dear Miss Richie Rich
You are a big sad bitch
Whose crotch will forever itch
And when you fart your pants unstitch

ANTHONY: They're not here. Cristina probably initiated a sweep of the upstairs.

Beat

ENZO: I'm gonna be a dad.

ANTHONY: I still can't believe it.

ENZO: We weren't trying. It just happened.

ANTHONY: You weren't "not" trying, though.

ENZO: Heh. Right. You and Cristina don't want—

ANTHONY: No.

ENZO: You'd be awesome parents.

ANTHONY: Probably.

ENZO: Do it. Join us.

ANTHONY: I believe in creating resources, not need.

ENZO: Babies *are* resources!

ANTHONY: I don't think anyone should have a child unless they're debt-free and have at least a quarter million, in cash, put aside for that child's medical needs and/or education and/or first home.

ENZO: We have free medicare and education.

ANTHONY: What if your kid gets really sick and needs some experimental treatment in the US? Or gets into an Ivy League school? Or wants to be an astronaut? How can you choose to be a parent and not provide the best possible opportunities for your child?

ENZO: Fuck, Ant, not for nothing but that's some snobby-ass garbage. If everyone waited to have a quarter million, that's—

ANTHONY: Two hundred and fifty K. Cash.

ENZO: Yeah. If you needed to have $250,000 to have a baby, then only rich people would have kids.

ANTHONY: I just solved the world's population problem, thank you very much.

ENZO: Parents don't owe their kids shit except love.

ANTHONY: It's the kids who shouldn't owe their parents anything. I always felt like I was paying off some debt, like they expected more and more. Rita always said, "Don't I deserve anything for having made you?"

ENZO: Bro, I have a serious question. Do you know what my face looks like right now?

ANTHONY: Yes. Like Dad's.

ENZO: Wait. Wait. Wait.

ENZO goes off into the junk, unseen.

ANTHONY: Where are you?

ANTHONY is not comfortable being alone. He glances at the painting. Gets stuck on it.

Before I met Cristina, I really couldn't see women. I couldn't relate to them, forget about being happy with someone. Men's faces were always easier for me. The features are sharper, more hard edges. They come into focus faster. For a long time, women were just bodies to me. Maybe that's why I never understood Rita.

ENZO emerges wearing his father's plumbing overalls. The name tag, Louie, stitched on.

ENZO: *(changing his voice)* Speaking, uh, of bodies, there is a fine piece of ass working at da gas station on Viau. Wanna make a stop at da pump, son?

ANTHONY: Enzo, what the fuck?

ENZO: You said when people change their clothes you get messed up.

ENZO pulls a piece of paper with a $100 bill clipped to it out of the breast pocket. He reads.

Pay Hydro. There it is! I'll do that tomorrow.

ANTHONY: Take that off.

ENZO: *(in Louie's voice)* You tink you're some big shot? Too busy for your own fadder. Da phone stuck to your goddamn head all da time, but you don't take my calls? You ungrateful shit. Dat's what you are. Mr. Lawyer too good for us.

ANTHONY: Should I be grateful that I paid my tuition with credit cards while you kept up your addiction to hookers and hoarding?

ENZO: Don't talk to me like dat no matter who you are in life!

Beat.

ANTHONY: Take that off. It's not funny.

ENZO does not remove the overalls.

ENZO: Why you getting like that for?

ANTHONY goes to get the papers.

ANTHONY: I did everything you wanted. Including some seriously stupid shit. Come sign these documents.

ENZO: Hey, Ant. Before we do all that I just want to say one thing.

ANTHONY: What now?

ENZO: Shit, I can't say it right, it's not gonna sound all eloquent and shit. But I'm so proud of everything you have going on. Driving by your election signs, seeing articles about you in the *Panoram*, the *Corriere*, the *Gazette* . . . that's pretty amazing. I wish you had shared more of it with us, but I understand why you didn't.

And I think you're going to be great. You're going to be the only honest politician out there.

> *Beat. It's like his dad is saying this for once.*

ANTHONY: Thank you.

ENZO: But you know, my two cents, you should be running here. St-Leonard will elect the red guy till the end of time.

ANTHONY: Enzo, have you actually read the articles or, you know, noticed the colours on my poster?

ENZO: What are you getting at?

ANTHONY: I'm running with the Conservative Party.

ENZO: What?! Does Cristina know that?

ANTHONY: It was a point of contention. I'm with the new wave of young conservatives. I'm socially liberal and fiscally conservative.

ENZO: Huh?

ANTHONY: Progressive on the issues, but careful with the spending.

ENZO: Meaning you love weed and hate poor people.

ANTHONY: This is the winning party. I can feel it. I can be in a position to create laws and not just interpret them. Like the anti-smoking legislation I helped pass.

ENZO: Seems to me you're a big bully for telling people what to do in their own house.

ANTHONY: If it's a multi-unit dwelling, it's a lot of people's homes. I plead that the good of the many outweighs the rights of a few.

ENZO: Shit. I wouldn't want to buy a freakin' anchovy tin to live in and then be bossed around by the other little fishies. Thank god I have this house.

ANTHONY: This house, Enzo—

ENZO: I want to own something that Nat can be proud of.

ANTHONY: You can own another house.

ENZO: I want *this* house. It's our home.

ANTHONY: I won't let you make that mistake. You finally have your life together. You're doing well. Don't jeopardize it with this—

ENZO: Are you punishing me?

ANTHONY: What?

ENZO: Cristina brought up the accident—

ANTHONY: What about it?

ENZO: She said it could be bad for your election or whatever.

ANTHONY: No worse than if they were alive.

ENZO: No, the other accident. The squeegee kid.

ANTHONY: Cristina said . . . Shit, I'm sorry . . . I told her not to—

ENZO: Yeah, or you're both playing this card making me feel like I owe you, just to convince me to do what you want with the house.

ANTHONY: FUCK, ENZO! Do you know the risk I took as an attorney?

ENZO: I made a mistake.

ANTHONY: You were drunk. You wrecked Dad's car. You damaged public property. You hit someone. And you fled the scene!

ENZO: I fled the scene? That was your advice. I wanted to stay, wait for the ambulance—

ANTHONY: You were wasted. I didn't know if the kid was dead. And with your prior "fuck the police" glowing record you would have been locked up a long time.

ENZO: I was just doing what you said.

ANTHONY: You were looking at criminal negligence, police fraud, and insurance fraud. And Dad too for lying for you.

ENZO: I know this.

ANTHONY: If it comes up for any reason during my campaign, you have to stick to the story.

ENZO: So it could be bad for you?

ANTHONY: It would end me.

Beat.

Tell me the story.

ENZO: Daddy was in bed. He didn't notice the car was missing until the next morning. He assumed our bitch neighbour Lucy had the car towed again for touching her side of the driveway. He was surprised when the police called. How'd I do?

ANTHONY: Really good.

ENZO: He wasn't hurt that bad, you know.

ANTHONY: Who?

ENZO: The squeegee. I went to visit him in the hospital.

ANTHONY: What!? You could have incriminated yourself.

ENZO: Relax. I pretended I was a church volunteer. Anyway, he was fine. Happy to be getting three meals and all that.

Beat.

Sometimes I wonder if you would have visited me more often if I went to jail.

ANTHONY: I couldn't be here for the three of you AND be available the way I wanted to be to Cristina and to my job.

Something needed to change.

ENZO: Well Mom and Dad are dead now. There's a change for you.

ANTHONY: It wasn't much of a change. They died. And I was hauled out of bed in the middle of the night to identify them—

ENZO: I told you. My phone was broken!

ANTHONY: And take care of it all. No end-of-life instructions, no funeral arrangements.

ENZO: End of life? What's that?

ANTHONY: Instructions as to how long you want to be kept alive artificially.

ENZO: They died from the accident.

ANTHONY: Dad passed at scene of the accident.

ENZO: And Mommy died at the hospital.

ANTHONY: She was in a coma, on a breathing machine, with serious brain inflammation. They had me choose between an aggressive intervention or sedation by painkillers.

ENZO: I wasn't a part of that decision.

ANTHONY: We couldn't reach you! A decision had to be made.

ENZO: So you killed her?

ANTHONY: I wanted to give her some dignity.

ENZO: You sure it wasn't revenge?

ANTHONY: Enzo, come on! This wasn't a choice between a fully functional life and death. It was choosing between a miserable, painful few days trapped in a lifeless body and death.

ENZO: She was Catholic. That wasn't what she wanted.

ANTHONY: Once again another huge decision was placed on my shoulders and rather than thank me—

ENZO: You want me to thank you for killing my mother?

ANTHONY: She was my mother too and I did the right thing!

ENZO: You were always so mean to her.

ANTHONY: I wasn't mean.

ENZO: You were cold.

ANTHONY: I was the only way I could be.

ENZO: She needed you.

ANTHONY: I can deal with anything. Confront anyone. Million-dollar court cases. Threats from big businessmen. Supreme Court judges examining my arguments. But I can't deal with them. I could vomit just thinking about having a conversation with them.

ENZO: Mommy was so proud of you. She talked about you all the time.

ANTHONY: I was just another thing to show off.

ENZO: So what's the difference when Cristina goes on about how perfect you are? Is she just showing off?

> *CRISTINA comes stumbling down the stairs with a drink in hand. She's wearing a long, flowing dress. The same one that Rita is wearing in the painting. The men don't notice her yet.*

ANTHONY: You mean because she makes that stupid joke about sculpting me? Maybe it's biological. Maybe women can't help but try to improve their partners. For the best chance of survival for their offspring. Not that Cristina was ever normal in that respect, not wanting children.

> *ANTHONY's phone starts ringing with Cecily's ringtone, in*
> *CRISTINA's hands. With her gaze set on ANTHONY, CRISTINA rejects*
> *the call.*

> *ANTHONY turns around and sees her in his mother's clothes.*

Okay. Why is everyone doing this to me today?

> *CRISTINA throws the phone at ANTHONY.*

CRISTINA: If you're going to treat me like your mother I may as well dress like her.

> *NAT comes down the stairs.*

NAT: I can't stop pissing. What I miss?

CRISTINA: Women are biologically designed to control and punish men.

ANTHONY: Our interview. You can't go like that! You look—

CRISTINA: WHAT. WHAT DO I LOOK LIKE ACCORDING TO YOU?

ANTHONY: You look like . . . like a miserable wretch addicted to pain, spreading that pain like a disease to everyone around you.

CRISTINA: What do *I* look like? Me! Do you see me? Do you see what I've given up for you?

ANTHONY: No. You don't get to resent me for a decision you made.

CRISTINA: I paused my life for this campaign.

ANTHONY: This campaign is just as much for you as it is for me. You needed a bigger stage, a larger audience.

CRISTINA: Yes, I need to be seen! I need . . .

ANTHONY: More. More than us. You were never satisfied with only two people in this marriage. I always had to share you with the whole world.

CRISTINA: Oh, please. What if you eloped with me because you hated your house and your family, and my parents were wealthy and you're a gold digger?

ANTHONY: If I'm a gold digger then you're a success digger. You love this, this power couple status.

CRISTINA: Is that so bad? Don't I deserve anything for having made you?

ANTHONY: Say that again. Put it in writing. I want to keep that.

CRISTINA: You set the bar so high, Anthony. Sometimes I think you want me to fail you so you can continue to prove the martyrdom of St. Anthony. But I refuse to fail you. I will not play that role in your self-fulfilling prophecy. I'm here. I chose you. I chose the sidecar.

Am I a bad feminist for doing that? And for never having sex with anyone but you?

She points at NAT.

She has slept with so many people!

CRISTINA crumples onto the sandbag and starts to cry.

NAT: What the hell, Crissy?

CRISTINA: *(weeping)* I keep wondering when you'll walk away. The way you left home without a second thought.

ANTHONY kneels down next to CRISTINA.

ANTHONY: You are the only home I've ever known.

CRISTINA: Rita said you'd leave me too. The way you left her.

ANTHONY: When did you talk to Rita?

CRISTINA: She said you take what you need from women and leave.

ANTHONY: When did you talk to my mother?

CRISTINA: I came here. Sometimes. I sat for the painting.

ANTHONY: That's you?

NAT: Not the face obviously. That's Rita.

ENZO: She put her face on Crissy's body.

ANTHONY: You had a relationship with my mother?

CRISTINA: I couldn't ignore her. It wasn't right.

ANTHONY: You know what's not right? Lying to your husband.

CRISTINA: I was so afraid that my husband hated women.

ANTHONY: I hated my mother. I don't hate women. Why can't there be a difference?

CRISTINA: You always defended your father; you blamed her for everything.

ENZO: It's true. I bet you wouldn't have pulled the plug on Daddy.

ANTHONY: Yes, I would have! I would pull the plug on everybody.

CRISTINA: You think she caused the accident. And you haven't cried yet. They've been dead for two weeks and you haven't cried.

ANTHONY: Crying is useless. It's nothing but emotional blackmail.

NAT: Enzo cries every night. Sometimes in the morning too.

ENZO: Babe, let's not intrude, okay?

CRISTINA: Why couldn't you just forgive her? Is it because you think forgiveness is weak? Your mom forgave your dad, over and over, so it must be the weak choice, the womanly choice.

ANTHONY: She didn't forgive. She never forgave, and she used me as . . . I can't believe you lied to me . . . I never ever . . . she poisons everything.

ANTHONY starts to hit himself on the head.

CRISTINA: Stop that!

ANTHONY: I have been yoked to this place since I was a child. I was the man of the house as a child. I don't forgive that.

CRISTINA: And only your mother could have prevented that?

ANTHONY: Isn't that what mothers are for?

CRISTINA: You were conditioned by our culture to believe that.

ANTHONY: Fuck, Cristina! You're nothing but a BuzzFeed feminist. No matter what, the woman is the victim, right? You are defending her right to be flawed, you are acknowledging that she was mistreated—but you're not listening to me!

CRISTINA: She was suffering. Just because you were able to convince your-self she didn't exist doesn't mean I could.

ANTHONY: You fell right into her trap. You let her manipulate you. She gets into your brain, that's what she does.

CRISTINA: She did not manipulate me.

ANTHONY: You know when painters figured out how to paint self-por-traits using mirrors? The fucking Renaissance!

CRISTINA: She was lonely. She needed me.

ANTHONY: What about me? I was a victim. ME!

ENZO: Ah fuck. I think you watched some *Dr. Phil* or some shit and con-fused it with our lives. I was there. You're exaggerating.

ANTHONY: All I ever wanted was for us to be normal. For there to be some kind of consistency to our lives. My nightmare? It's always the same. I'm lying in bed and all this stuff—THIS STUFF—is piled on my chest and I can't breathe. I try to get it off but it's too heavy. It's pushing down on me and the objects are not just objects, they're cold, hard misery and sadness and pain. When I wake up, I know the weight isn't on me anymore but every time I'm reminded that all that misery and sadness and pain is stuck to my skin.

ANTHONY goes to get the statue of Lady Justice that he picked up toward the beginning of the play.

You see this? When I passed the bar, Rita and Louie gave me this statue and Rita said, "We're so proud. Now all our financial problems are over." My achievement became another way to help this family. It wasn't for me. It was for them. In the moment of my biggest accomplishment, I suddenly wasn't sure if I did it because I wanted to do it or because I felt an obligation to do it. We can't make our progeny into our saviours. That's the whole fucking problem with the Jesus myth.

CRISTINA: You would have been such a good father.

ANTHONY: You can't raise your child here.

ENZO: STOP TELLING ME WHAT TO DO.

ANTHONY: *(to NAT)* Let's be real, Nat. There's a good chance that baby is going to end up in a basket on my doorstep. You want to save some time and draw up the adoption papers now?

NAT: Hold the goddamn phone, asshole.

CRISTINA: He's not serious.

ANTHONY: We're the only ones who can raise that baby with some stability.

ENZO: You're really full of it, you know that?

NAT: You don't know me. I would never abandon my kid.

ANTHONY: *(to ENZO)* Is the kid going to eat Doritos for dinner?

ENZO: No.

ANTHONY: *(to ENZO)* Be forced to go on plumbing jobs with you when he's eight?

ENZO: No.

ANTHONY: Trip over the junk on these stairs, break his leg, and wait three hours for you to pick him up from the ER?

ENZO: Stop.

ANTHONY: Oh, and is he going to remember do all his sixth-grade home-work and pay the utility bills on time? He's not going to study for the bar exam in the cold by candlelight, is he?

ENZO: This is not going to be like us.

ANTHONY: I'm not convinced. What do you think, Cristina? Wanna adopt?

CRISTINA: Enough, Anthony. You made your point.

ANTHONY: Should we turn the office into a nursery? It won't have the dilapidated charm of this place, but—

NAT: Hey! This baby belongs to me! You're not that old; have your own.

CRISTINA: We're a dink family. Remember? DINK!

ENZO: What the fuck is a dink?

CRISTINA: Anyway, we can't. Anthony had a vasectomy.

ENZO: Wow, Ant. You hated us so much you had to get the big snip to make sure our DNA would never bother you again.

CRISTINA: I knew it. I knew you'd regret it.

ANTHONY: I don't regret it. You wanted to do the show.

CRISTINA: So you had a vasectomy to punish me for putting my career first?

ANTHONY: I did it so you'd never have to make that choice again. And then you quit the show.

CRISTINA: I thought you didn't want children.

ANTHONY: I didn't. Most of the time.

Beat.

ENZO: I bet you have everything on your parenting checklist, right, Ant? You have that two hundred K all saved up, unlike your idiot brother who thinks all babies need is love—

ANTHONY: Stop it. Stop being proud of having nothing and think for a minute about what's better for that child. Now that it's too late for an abortion.

ENZO: What did you just say?

> *ENZO lunges at ANTHONY and throws a few punches. They grapple to the ground. ANTHONY grabs the statue.*

You'll never be a father. That's why you're acting like such a little cunt. Who's the man of the house now?

NAT: Stop!

ENZO: This is my house! I stayed! You left!

ANTHONY: Yes, I left, and you should have too!

ENZO: You act ashamed of us, but you're ashamed of yourself.

ANTHONY: I have nothing to be ashamed of.

ENZO: They needed you here. You killed them, Ant, you did it! They died of broken hearts.

ANTHONY is at his breaking point. He lifts the statue up to strike ENZO with it. He stops and starts to weep. ENZO embraces him.

ANTHONY: Why won't you just leave? Leave this place. I want to be your brother. I love you—I love you—but I can't be here.

ENZO: I don't throw things away.

ANTHONY: All I want is to take care of the people I love.

ENZO looks at ANTHONY for a beat.

ENZO: Me too.

ENZO stands up.

I know what's best for my family. I want to raise my kid here. I have some money to buy you out—

ANTHONY: You can't live here.

ANTHONY stays on the ground for a beat, takes his puffer, then stands.

CRISTINA: There is no "buyout." This place is a liability. There's more debt than equity.

ANTHONY: If you took possession of the place, you'd be taking on the debts.

ANTHONY goes to get the papers on the desk.

ENZO: Let me see those.

ENZO takes the papers and reads.

ANTHONY: That's the liability on the house. Two bank mortgages, a private lender, and a lien. It's worthless.

ENZO: . . . Five hundred K . . . Half a million.

ANTHONY: We won't have to take responsibility for any of it once we sign this document issued to successors.

ANTHONY hands ENZO another document.

ENZO: I renounce. I renounce. I hereby renounce. What the fuck? You highlighted them all for me to sign. Not "I accept, I accept, I accept." You forgot to highlight those options? You made my decision for me.

ANTHONY: A renunciation of the succession means we're not liable for any debts. The lenders will come and repossess the house.

ENZO: Our house.

ANTHONY: There's nothing left of it.

ENZO: What do you mean? It's right here! We're standing in it. So what if there's a little debt?

ANTHONY: It's a half-million dollars.

ENZO: Big businessmen owe millions! Ask your father-in-law.

ANTHONY: This place is not worth it. It's falling apart and you will never ever crawl out from under the weight of this debt. Your child will never be free of it.

NAT: So let the bank take it and then Enzo can buy it cheap at auction. I saw that on—

ANTHONY: This is not TLC!

ENZO: Meaning what?

ANTHONY: It's complicated. Just take my word for it.

ENZO: No. I won't take your word. I think this is about you making sure this place disappears. You finally get what you always wanted.

ANTHONY: I am giving you the most sensible legal advice. I would give this advice to my most valued client.

ENZO: I want to raise my family here.

ANTHONY: Poor and stupid? You want to keep the cycle going?

ENZO: Fuck you. You're not who you think you are. You're just a wop who jumped the fence.

ANTHONY: You're right. I do want this place gone. I want every trace of it gone so it will never embarrass me again.

ANTHONY takes out his chequebook.

How much money do you want to walk away?

ENZO: I am not going to walk away. Keep your money.

NAT: Enzo, not so fast. Maybe you do want his money, but not to walk away. To cover the debt.

CRISTINA: Oh come on, Nat. A half-million dollars? You want to ease your guilt, not the debt. Just admit that you don't want to live together.

NAT: *(to CRISTINA)* Fuck you!

ENZO: What?

NAT: Not right away. I need time.

ANTHONY: That is not the deal I offered. I am not paying off the debt on this house.

ENZO: *(quietly)* Anthony.

ANTHONY: No, Enzo.

ENZO: You probably don't want me talking about the squeegee to any journalists.

> Beat. *This is hard for* ENZO.

ANTHONY: Are you blackmailing me?

ENZO: Anything for my kid, right?

ANTHONY: Enzo, come on.

ENZO: I'm no lawyer, but that can't be up to par with your code of ethics, can it?

ANTHONY: I could be disbarred.

CRISTINA: Stop. Everyone needs to stop talking.

ENZO: And who would vote for you then?

ANTHONY: I did what I did that night because I care about you. The same reason I'm doing this.

ENZO: How can that be? You don't have time for emotion.

ANTHONY: What if I renounce my part and you keep 100% of the succession?

ENZO: Sure.

ANTHONY: You will be 100% responsible for the debt.

ENZO: But you're going to help me out with that.

ANTHONY: Even if I could give you five-hundred grand, which I can't, you have to understand it doesn't end there. You'll be liable to other creditors suing the estate.

ENZO: Make me an offer.

ANTHONY: I would draft a strict non-disclosure agreement.

ENZO: Understood. Make me an offer.

CRISTINA: What the fuck is going on? Why are we in a gangster movie all of a sudden?

ANTHONY: One hundred and fifty K.

CRISTINA: What? The campaign is already costing us—

ENZO: Shut up, Cristina. It's obvious your father's paying for the campaign with his filthy money.

ANTHONY: One hundred and fifty thousand dollars. I'll call my banker first thing tomorrow.

ENZO: Make it a quarter million. In case my baby wants to be an astronaut.

NAT: *(to ENZO)* Is that enough?

ENZO: I'm no thief. Let's call it your half of the debt.

ANTHONY: Understand that if I give you this money, you will never see me again.

ENZO: That's fair.

ANTHONY: Done.

ENZO: Let's shake on it.

    ENZO holds out his hand. There is a long beat. ANTHONY shakes.

Is this my copy of the documents?

ANTHONY: Yes.

ENZO: How long do I have?

ANTHONY: Sixty days. That's also how long undiscovered creditors have to come forward. Consider that one last bit of legal advice. I'm renouncing first thing in the morning.

ENZO: I'll mail my completed acceptance papers to your office. I'll even use a stamp so as not to embarrass you.

CRISTINA: Come on, you're brothers. This is not right.

ENZO: Some things you inherit without a choice and some things you choose. You can choose to forget all of this, Anthony. I won't judge you for that. You'll even forget my face soon enough.

ANTHONY: Cristina, let's go.

    CRISTINA walks up to the painting. She takes a hold of it and is going to drag it out with her.

ENZO: Everything stays.

CRISTINA: This painting means a lot to me.

NAT: Let her have it. It's her body after all.

CRISTINA: Thank you, Nat.

ANTHONY: No.

CRISTINA starts to lift the canvas. ANTHONY locks eyes with her. ANTHONY leaves. CRISTINA looks like she's going to shatter right there. She leaves the painting, nods at NAT, and leaves.

NAT and ENZO stand in silence for a beat.

ENZO: Babe, I know you're not sure. And that's okay. But in the meantime, I am going to build you such a beautiful house. What do you want? Anything. Name it.

NAT: I . . . don't know . . . I never really thought about it.

ENZO: Come on. You have.

NAT: Maybe a shower—a really big shower—with one of those rainforest heads.

ENZO grabs one of the big lead pipes and goes off into another room.

Where you going?

NAT waits. Nothing. She picks up the box of pastries and walks over to the painting. She studies it while eating. Very loud smashing sounds are heard. NAT is startled.

Enzo?

ENZO comes back on.

What was that?

ENZO: I smashed all the tiles in the bathroom. Tomorrow I'll start building your shower.

NAT: Maybe a nursery should come first.

ENZO: Right. Yeah.

NAT: We can hang this painting in the baby's room.

ENZO: We'll tell him his grandmother was a talented painter and his great-grandfather and his grandfather were plumbers just like Daddy.

NAT: His?

ENZO: I really think so. I can feel it. Little Louie Jr. Next comes Rita.

ENZO hugs NAT from behind, his hands on her belly. So much for Nat Jr.

ACKNOWLEDGEMENTS

This play was first developed as part of Infinithéâtre's 2015/2016 Playwrighting Unit, under Guy Sprung's artistic direction and Alexandria Haber's dramaturgy. The play would not have been possible without my cohort's input that year. Thank you to the unit: Alison Darcy, Joanna Gosse, Travis Martin, Stephen Orlov, Patrick Pietrykowski, Joseph Shragge, and (with fond remembrance) Joel Yanofsky.

Thank you to Roy Surette for programming the first public reading at Centaur Theatre and for programming the play's world premiere in his final season. Thank you to Eda Holmes for immediately supporting this play and me as a playwright.

Thank you to Playwrights' Workshop Montréal and Emma Tibaldo, who supported the second phase of dramaturgy and development for this play.

I am so grateful to the cast. Thank you to Carlo for bringing reason, justice, and vulnerability to Anthony. Thank you, Davide, for showing Enzo's heart, wit, and optimism. Thank you, Gita, for embodying the grace, steely determination, and self-assuredness that is—and that saves—Nat. Tara, only you could play Cristina. Only you could understand the neuroses and the love that guides her. You have always said yes to me and your impact on my life has made me a better human and artist. Micheline, thank you for your guidance and for looking me in the eye at the end of the process and calling me "a true person of the theatre."

Tamara, I had never felt so seen as I did when I heard your belly laughs in the audience during my first production of *8 Ways*. Thank you for making space for me exactly as I am and for being the one who "called it" first. If any of this happened, it was to vindicate you.

Michaela Di Cesare is a playwright and performer with an M.A. in drama from the University of Toronto. Her solo show, *8 Ways My Mother Was Conceived* was presented across Canada and in New York City. Next came *In Search of Mrs. Pirandello* at Centaur Theatre's 2016 Wildside Festival, followed by the main stage world premiere of *Successions* in the 2017/2018 season. *Extra/ Beautiful/U* won first place in the 2017 Write-on-Q competition presented by Infinithéâtre. *FOMO (Fear of Missing Out)* premiered with Geordie Productions in September 2019 (Outstanding New Text Nomination, METAS 2020). Michaela was playwright-in-residence at Centaur Theatre in 2019/2020, writing *Terroni or Once Upon a Time in the South*. She is currently working on a new play, *Hot Blooded Foreigner* for Tableau D'Hôte Theatre and several projects for film and television.

First edition: March 2022
Printed and bound in Canada by Imprimerie Gauvin, Gatineau

Jacket design by Angelina Doherty
Author photo © Julian Stamboulieh

202-269 Richmond St. W.
Toronto, ON
M5V 1X1

416.703.0013
info@playwrightscanada.com
www.playwrightscanada.com
@playcanpress